An Edwardian Carol Book

An Edwardian Carol Book

12 CAROLS FOR MIXED VOICES

Selected and edited by Jeremy Dibble

MUSIC DEPARTMENT

OXFORD
UNIVERSITY PRESS

OXFORD
UNIVERSITY PRESS

198 Madison Avenue, New York, NY 10016, USA
Great Clarendon Street, Oxford OX2 6DP, England

Oxford University Press is a department of the University of Oxford.
It furthers the University's aim of excellence in research, scholarship,
and education by publishing worldwide

Oxford New York
Auckland Cape Town Hong Kong Karachi
Kuala Lumpur Madrid Melbourne Mexico City Nairobi
New Delhi Shanghai Taipei Toronto

With offices in

Argentina Austria Brazil Chile Czech Republic France Greece
Guatemala Hungary Italy Japan Poland Portugal Singapore
South Korea Switzerland Thailand Turkey Ukraine Vietnam

Oxford is a registered trademark of Oxford University Press

1 3 5 7 9 10 8 6 4 2

ISBN 0–19–386966–7 978–0–19–386966–0

Music and text engraving by
Barnes Music Engraving Ltd., East Sussex, England

Printed in the United States on acid-free paper

CONTENTS

INTRODUCTION

For the revival of the Christmas carol in the nineteenth century we should look to two Cornish antiquarians, Davies Gilbert (who published *Some Ancient Christmas Carols* in 1822) and William Sandys (whose *Christmas Carols, Ancient and Modern* appeared in 1833). Their work was adapted by a number of successors, among them J. M. Neale and Thomas Helmore (their *Carols for Christmas-tide* of 1853–4, from *Piae Cantiones* of 1582), Edmund Sedding (his nine *Antient Christmas Carols* of 1860), Joshua Sylvester (*A Garland of Christmas Carols Ancient and Modern* of 1861), Edward Francis Rimbault (*A Collection of Old Christmas Carols* and *A Little Book of Christmas Carols* of 1861 and 1863 respectively), and William Husk (*Songs of the Nativity: being Christmas Carols, Ancient & Modern* of 1864).

But it was in 1867, with the publication of the first series of 20 *Christmas Carols New and Old* by John Stainer and his Magdalen colleague, the Rev. Henry Ramsden Bramley, that the carol began to establish itself as part of the Victorian Christmas. Two further series were published in 1871 (22 carols) and 1878 (28) bringing the total to 70, and this collection became the staple diet of many a church and domestic fireside. Stainer's musical arrangements were entirely pragmatic. Their simple harmonizations, highly adaptable and expertly crafted for accompaniment on the organ or piano, were intended for the archetypal parish church choir or even for the drawing-room, while the subject matter of the carols themselves was uncontroversial, popular, and eminently performable. Many of the carols were traditional (including such favorites as "The First Nowell" and "God rest ye merry, gentlemen"), but Stainer also used the opportunity to invite his contemporaries to write new works for the collection, among them John Bacchus Dykes and Joseph Barnby. Cathedrals, which had shown little interest in carols, began steadily to include them in the octave of Christmas during the 1870s, and Stainer, in particular, encouraged their performance at St Paul's Cathedral after 1877. By the end of the nineteenth century the appetite for Christmas carols began to burgeon, and while Stainer's and Bramley's collection remained very popular throughout the Edwardian era (four carols from the collection, by Stainer, Dykes, and Barnby are represented here), antiquarians such as the Rev. G. R. Woodward led the harvesting of carols from continental sources and musical editors such as Stainer, George Martin, and Charles Wood arranged the melodies. Parallel with this enthusiasm for new material was the production of contemporary original carols from composers who enjoyed their heyday at the end of Victoria's reign and that of Edward VII.

Stanford produced a number of carols for the Christmas season. "As with gladness men of old" was first published as an "Extra Supplement" for the *Musical Times* in 1894 and also appeared under the name "Orient" in the *Methodist Hymn Book* of 1904. "A Carol for Christmas" appeared as the first piece in his third set of *Six Elizabethan Pastorales* Op. 67 (1897), written for and dedicated to Lionel Benson and the Magpie Madrigal Society, at that time one of the foremost choirs specializing in unaccompanied choral music. Houghton & Co. published "A Carol of the Nativity" in 1909, and by special arrangement with the publisher, the *Daily Express* printed it as a "New Christmas Carol for Express Readers" on 9 December that same year. Elgar's "Lo! Christ the Lord is born" was composed in 1897 as a private Christmas card but it was not published until 1909. His setting of Ben Jonson's "I sing the birth" was completed on 30 October

1928 and first performed at the Royal Albert Hall by the Royal Choral Society under the direction of Malcolm Sargent. The Royal Choral Society, under the direction of Sir Frederick Bridge, was the recipient of all three carols by Parry, who composed them during the dark days of World War I. The first, "When Christ was born of Mary free," was sung at the Royal Albert Hall at the choir's Christmas concert on 18 December 1915. "I sing the birth" and "Welcome, Yule!" were published together as *Two Carols* by Novello; both, according to the composer, were sung with great spirit by the same choir at the same venue on 17 December 1917.

A Note on the Editorial Policy

The printed sources of these carols have been used as the principal sources for this edition. Older notational practices have been altered to conform with modern notational practices, and open-score format has, in some cases, been re-originated to two staves. Where accents or dynamics only appear in one part, but are clearly missing in the others, these have been added for consistency and clarity without comment. All editorial dynamics have been added in square brackets and editorial slurs are shown with an additional slash. The small inconsistency in Elgar's "I sing the birth" (beats 3 and 4 of mm. 10 – ♩ ♪ – and 46 – ♩. ♪) has been reconciled to the version in m. 10. Furthermore, Elgar's pause on beat 3 of m. 66 has been replaced by a comma. In some of the carols, verse numbers are missing, so these have been added to aid rehearsal. In Stanford's "A Carol of the Nativity," the organ, which enters in verse 6, may be used to accompany the choir throughout; a similar practice may be applied to Dykes's "Sleep, Holy Babe!" For Stainer's "The Child Jesus in the Garden," a short introduction and interlude between verses for the organ have been added by the editor. These may be omitted in performance if wished.

JEREMY DIBBLE
Durham, 2006

List of Sources

1. A Carol for Christmas
Music: Charles Villiers Stanford; Text: Edmund Bolton; Source: No. 1 of *Six Elizabethan Pastorales* Op. 67, Boosey, 1897.

2. A Carol of the Nativity
Music: Charles Villiers Stanford; Text: Arthur Cleveland Coxe; Source: E. Houghton & Co., 1909; also published by the *Daily Express* as a "New Christmas Carol for Express Readers," 9 December 1909. Reprinted by Novello, 1913.

3. A Cradle-song of the Blessed Virgin
Music: Joseph Barnby; Text: from the Latin trans. by Rev. H. R. Bramley; Source: No. XXXIII in Stainer and Bramley (eds.) *Christmas Carols New and Old* (Series II), Novello, 1871.

4. As with gladness men of old
Music: Charles Villiers Stanford; Text: W. Chatterton Dix; Source: Novello, 1894; also *Musical Times* Extra Supplement, December 1894 and *Novello's Christmas Carols* No. 217. The tune was also known by the name of "Orient."

5. Christmas Song
Music: John Bacchus Dykes; Text: William Bright; Source: No. XXXIV in Stainer and Bramley (eds.) *Christmas Carols New and Old* (Series II), Novello, 1871.

6. I sing the birth
Music: Edward Elgar; Text: Ben Jonson (with "Alleluias" added); Source: Novello, 1928.

7. I sing the birth
Music: C. Hubert H. Parry; Text: Ben Jonson; Source: Novello, 1917.

8. Lo! Christ the Lord is born
Music: Edward Elgar; Text: Shapcott Wensley; Source: composed in 1897; published by Novello, 1909.

9. Sleep, Holy Babe!
Music: John Bacchus Dykes; Text: Edward Caswall; Source: No. IX in Stainer and Bramley (eds.) *Christmas Carols New and Old* (Series I), Novello, 1867.

10. The Child Jesus in the Garden
Music: John Stainer; Text: John Stainer; Source: in Stainer and Bramley (eds.) *Christmas Carols New and Old* (Series II), Novello 1871.

11. Welcome, Yule!
Music: C. Hubert H. Parry; Text: 15th century; Source: Novello, 1917.

12. When Christ was born of Mary free
Music: C. Hubert H. Parry; Text: 15th century; Source: Novello, 1915.

for my friend, Giles Brightwell

1. A Carol for Christmas

Edmund Bolton
(1575?–1633?)

CHARLES V. STANFORD
(1852–1924)

Printed in USA

flock of stars hath pent, That we might them be-hold. Yet, from their beams pro-ceed-eth

not— this light, Nor can— their crys-tals such— re - flec-tion give. What then doth

make the el - e-ments so bright?— The hea-vens are— come down on earth to

live. But heark - en to the song:— 'Glo - ry to

Glory's King! And peace— all men a - mong!'— These

Glo - ry to

2. A Carol of the Nativity

Arthur Cleveland Coxe
(1818–96)

CHARLES V. STANFORD
(1852–1924)

1. Ca - rol, sweet - ly ca - rol, Sing most joy - ful - ly;

Ca - rol of the com-ing Of Christ's Na - ti - vi-ty; Pray a glad-some Christ-mas

For all Chris-tian men: Gath - er here in glad-ness, For Christ-mas comes a-gain.

The organ, which enters in verse 6, may be used to accompany throughout.

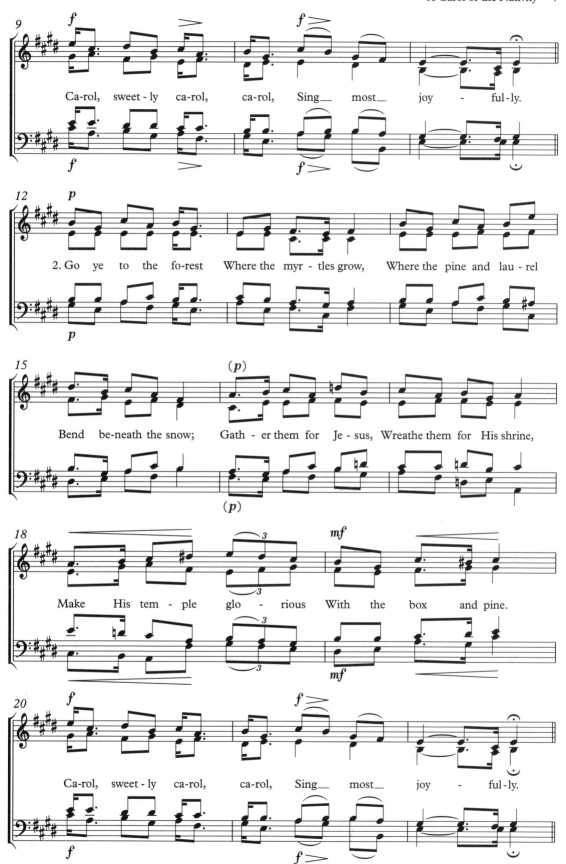

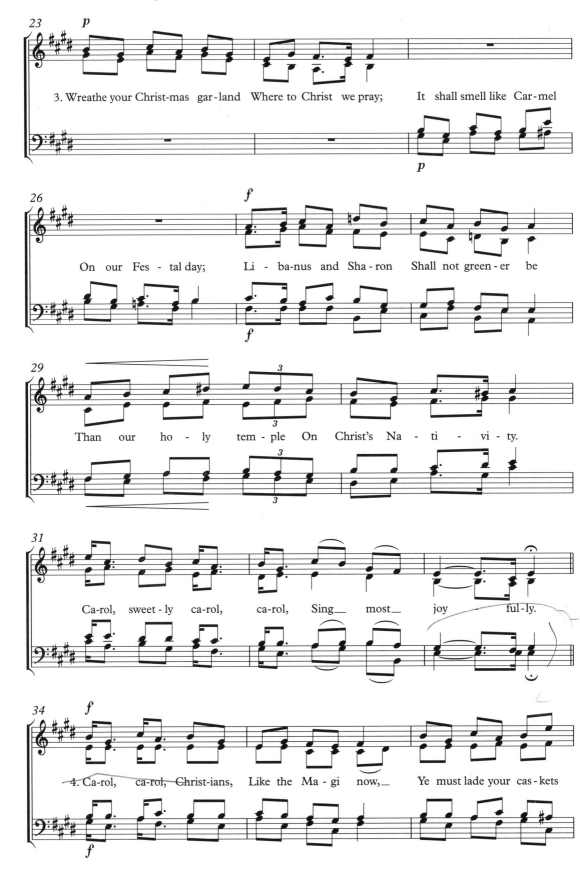

3. Wreathe your Christ-mas gar-land Where to Christ we pray; It shall smell like Car-mel On our Fes - tal day; Li - ba-nus and Sha - ron Shall not green - er be Than our ho - ly tem - ple On Christ's Na - ti - vi - ty. Ca-rol, sweet - ly ca-rol, ca-rol, Sing___ most___ joy ___ ful - ly.

4. Ca-rol, ca-rol, Christ-ians, Like the Ma - gi now,___ Ye must lade your cas - kets

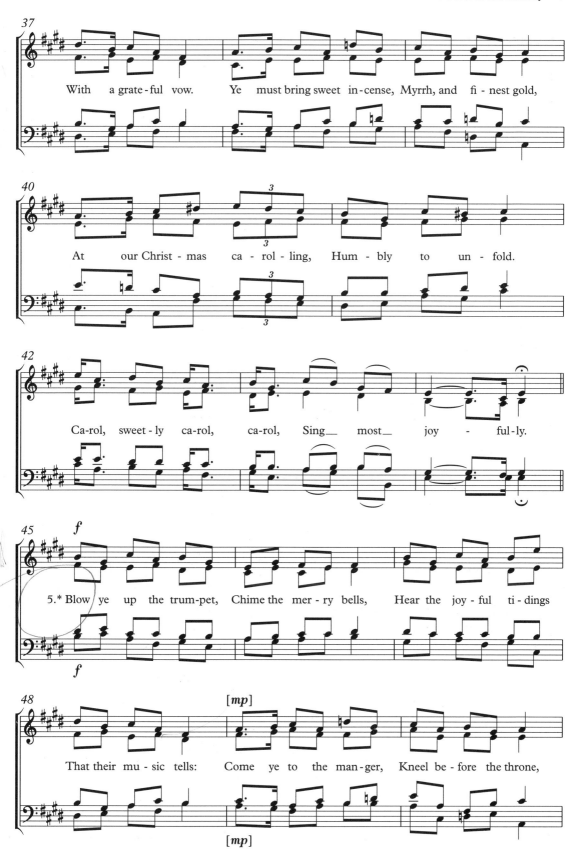

37

With a grate-ful vow. Ye must bring sweet in-cense, Myrrh, and fi-nest gold,

40

At our Christ-mas ca-rol-ling, Hum-bly to un-fold.

42

Ca-rol, sweet-ly ca-rol, ca-rol, Sing__ most__ joy - ful-ly.

45 *f*

5.* Blow ye up the trum-pet, Chime the mer-ry bells, Hear the joy-ful ti-dings

f

48 [*mp*]

That their mu-sic tells: Come ye to the man-ger, Kneel be-fore the throne,

[*mp*]

* The text of v. 5 was rewritten by H. F. Manly.

Hail   the blest   Re - deem - er,   Claim Him   as   your   own.

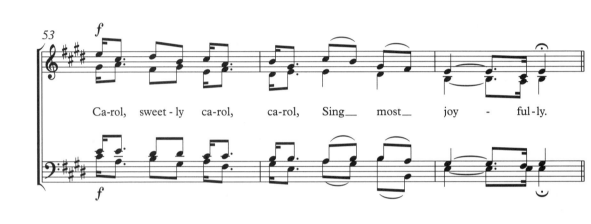

Ca-rol,   sweet - ly   ca-rol,   ca-rol,   Sing__   most__   joy -   ful - ly.

6. Give us grace, O   Sa-viour,   To put off in might   Deeds and dreams of dark-ness,

ORG.

Ped.

For the robes of light, And to live as low-ly As Thy-self with men,

So to rise in glo - ry When Thou com'st a - gain.

[a tempo]
Ca-rol, sweet-ly ca-rol, ca-rol, Sing_ most_ joy - ful-ly.

[a tempo]

3. A Cradle-song of the Blessed Virgin

Words translated from the
Latin by Rev. H. R. Bramley (1833–1917)

JOSEPH BARNBY
(1838–96)

Allegretto non troppo

3. My Child, of Might in - dwell - ing, My
4. My Joy, my Ex - ul - ta - tion, My
5. Say, wouldst Thou hea - venly sweet - ness Or

Sweet, all sweets ex - cell - ing, Of Bliss the Foun - tain
spi - rit's Con - so - la - tion; My Son, my Spouse, my
love of an - swering meet - ness? Or is fit mu - sic

più lento

flow - ing, The Day - spring ev - er glow - ing._____
Bro - ther, O lis - ten to Thy Mo - ther._____ My
want - ing? Ho! An - gels raise your chant - ing!_____

Dar - ling, do not weep, My Je - su, sleep!_____

4. As with gladness men of old

W. Chatterton Dix
(1837–98)

CHARLES V. STANFORD
(1852–1924)

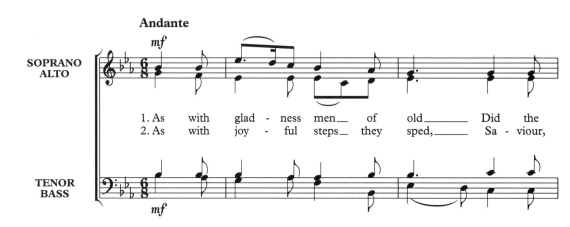

1. As with glad - ness men of old Did the
2. As with joy - ful steps they sped, Sa - viour,

guid - ing star be - hold, As with joy they hail'd its
to Thy low - ly bed, There to bend the knee be -

light, Lead - ing on - ward, beam - ing bright;
- fore Thee Whom heaven and earth a - dore;

So, most gra - cious Lord,__ may we_____ Ev - er - more,
So may we_____ with will - ing feet_____ E - ver seek,

ev - er - more__ be led_____ to Thee.
e - ver seek__ the mer - - cy - seat.

3. As they of - fered gifts__ most rare_____ At Thy
4. Ho - ly Je - sus, ev - ery day_____ Keep us

cra - dle rude__ and bare; So may we_____ with ho - ly
in the nar - row way; And, when earth - ly things are

20

joy,_____ Pure   and   free____ from sin's   al -   loy,_____
past,_____ Bring   our   ran - somed souls   at   last_____

23 *f*

All   our   cost - liest   trea - sures bring,____ Christ,   to Thee,
Where   they   need____ no   star____ to   guide,____ Where   no clouds,

f

26 *dim.*   *p*

Christ,   to   Thee____ our   heaven -   -   ly   King.
where   no   clouds__ Thy   glo -   -   ry   hide.

dim.   *p*

(28) *mf*

5. In   the   heaven - ly   coun - try   bright_____ Need   they

mf

5. Christmas Song

William Bright
(1824–1901)

JOHN BACCHUS DYKES
(1823–76)

26   *mf*

4. Yea,__ if o - thers stand__ a - part,_____ We__ will press__ the__
5. So__ we yield__ Thee all__ we can,_____ Wor - ship, thanks, and__
6. Thou__ that once,__ 'mid sta - ble cold,_____ Wast__ in babe - clothes

mf

29

near - er:_____ Yea,__ O best__ fra - ter - nal Heart, We will
bless - ing;_____ Thee__ true God,__ and Thee__ true Man, On our
ly - ing,_____ Thou__ whose Al - tar - veils__ en - fold, Power and

32

hold__ Thee dear - - er, We will__ hold_____ Thee
knees__ con - fess - - ing, On our__ knees_____ con -
Life__ un - dy - - ing, Power and__ Life_____ un -

35   *p*

dear - - er;_____ Faith - ful lips shall an - swer thus____
- fess - - ing;_____ While Thy Birth - day morn__ we greet____
- dy - - ing,_____ Thou whose Love be - stows__ a worth____

p

To all faith - less scorn - ing,   'Je - sus Christ is
With our best de - vo - tion,   Bathe us, O most
On each poor en - dea - vour,   Have Thou joy of

God__ with us,   Born on Christ - mas morn - ing,____
true__ and sweet!   In Thy mer - cy's o - cean,____
this__ Thy Birth   In our praise_ for ev - er,____

Born__ on Christ - mas morn - - - ing,____
In__ thy mer - cy's o - - - cean,____
In__ our praise_ for ev - - - er,____

Born__ on__ Christ - mas__ morn - - ing.'
In__ thy__ mer - cy's__ o - - cean.
In__ our__ praise_ for__ ev - - er.

to my friend The Rev. Harcourt B. S. Fowler, Elmley Castle, Worcestershire

6. I sing the birth

Ben Jonson (1573–1637)
(with 'Alleluias' added)

EDWARD ELGAR
(1857–1934)

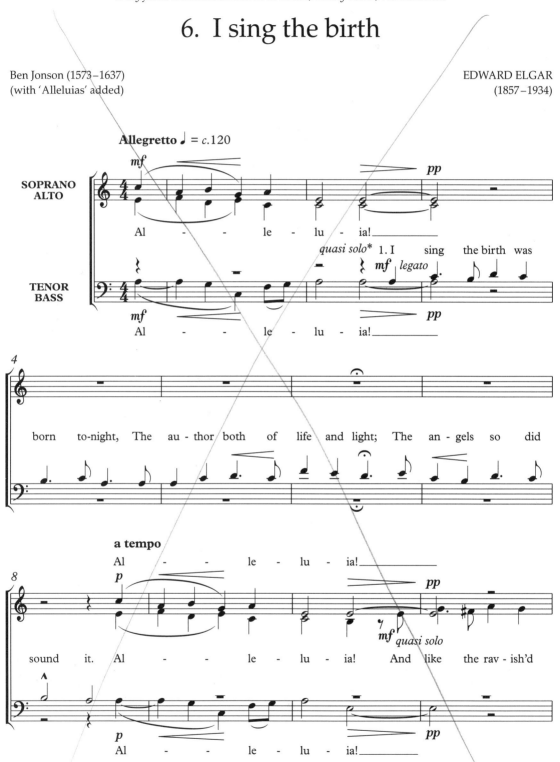

* These passages should be sung in a very free manner, without any rigid adherence to tempo. They may be taken by solo voices if desired.

7. I sing the birth

Ben Jonson
(1573–1637)

C. HUBERT H. PARRY
(1848–1918)

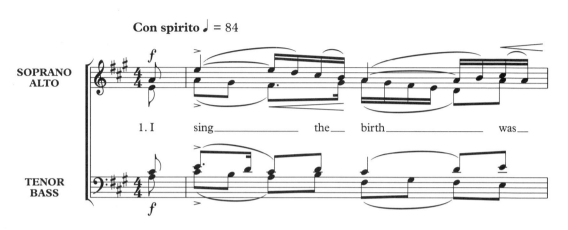

1. I sing_____ the__ birth_____ was__

born_____ to-night, The au - thor__ both_____ of__

life_____ and light; The an - gels__ so_____ did__

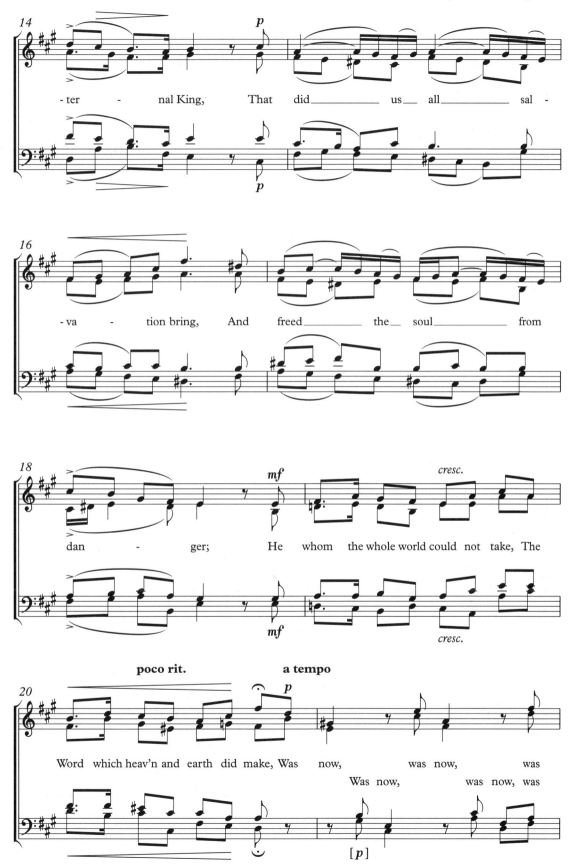

- ter - nal King, That did____ us_ all____ sal -

- va - tion bring, And freed____ the_ soul____ from

dan - ger; He whom the whole world could not take, The

poco rit.   **a tempo**

Word which heav'n and earth did make, Was now,   was now,   was

Was now,   was now, was

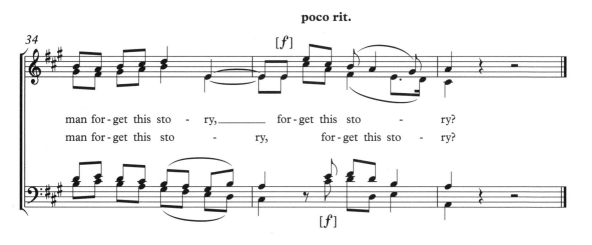

8. Lo! Christ the Lord is born

Shapcott Wensley

EDWARD ELGAR
(1857–1934)

9. Sleep, Holy Babe!

Edward Caswall
(1814–78)

JOHN BACCHUS DYKES
(1823–76)

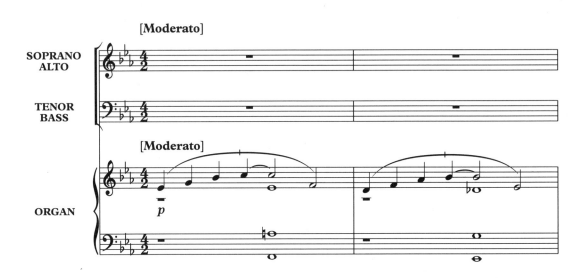

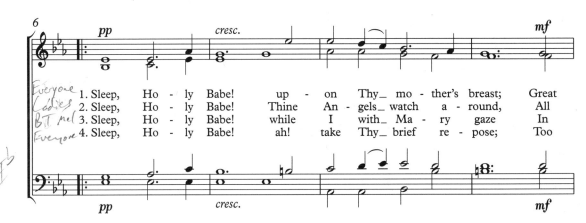

The organ may accompany the voices throughout.

10. The Child Jesus in the Garden

Words and music by
JOHN STAINER
(1840–1901)

Performers may omit some verses if they choose.

1. in a gar - den bare,_____ Walked the Child_____
2. missed with - in His home,_____ His_____ Mo - ther
6. smile of love so deep,_____ Win - ter him -
~~in these Christ~~ - mas hours,_____ Sor - row, like_____

1. Je - sus wrapt_ in ho - ly_____ thought;
2. gen - tle marked His ev - ery_____ way:
6. - self grew warm_ be - neath____ its_____ glow,
~~snow, will melt,~~ if He_____ but_____ smile;

1. His   brow   seemed cloud -   ed   with   a   weight   of
2. Forth   then   she   came   to   seek   where He ___ did
6. From   droop - ing   bran - ches   scent - ed   blos - soms
   And   if   He   clothe   thy   win - try   path ___ with

1. care, _____   Calm - ness   and   rest   from world - ly
2. roam, _____   Full ___ of   sweet words   His   trou - ble
6. peep, _____   Up ___ springs the   grass, the   seal - èd
   flowers, _____ A - midst ___ thy ___ mirth, think on   His

* Organ double voices ad lib. in vv. 3, 5, 7, and 9.

Forc - ing her____ way 'mid bran - ches black____ and____ sere;
Long - ing to____ melt His look_ of sad - dest____ grief,
Off - 'ring to____ Him the fra - grance of____ their____ store;
Yet on His____ brow He placed it, full____ of____ joy;

Hast - 'ning, that she His sor - rows might_ di - vide,____
With lift - ed eyes His ear to her____ He lent;____
Chant - ing sweet notes the birds a - round Him fly,____
Full well He knew why He on earth_ was born,____

Share____ all His woe, or calm His gloom - y fear.
Her____ kind - ly so - lace brought His soul re - lief.
Wond - 'ring why earth had che - quered so her floor.
How____ by His blood He should our woes de - stroy.

on to vv. 4 & 8
back to vv. 6 & 10 (p. 36)

mp

dim.

46

SOLO S. / T.

mp

4. 'Speak, gen - tle Lord;'_____ she cried with rev - erent love,_____
8. Then round His Mo - ther li - lies white en - twined,_____

mp

50

v. 8:

'Tell me, I_____ pray, what griefs a - round_____ Thee_____ press,
Fresh as her_____ love, and chaste as she_____ was_____ pure;

A -

54

Though I of earth, and Thou from Heaven a - bove,_____
- bout His_____ head the Pas - sion-flowers did bind,_____

58

back to vv. 5 & 9 (p. 39)

I am Thy Mo - ther: what doth Thee dis - tress?'
Type of the suf - f'rings He must soon en - dure.

42

11. Welcome, Yule!

Words: 15th cent.

C. HUBERT H. PARRY
(1848–1918)

Copyright © 2006, Oxford University Press Inc.

* in company

12. When Christ was born of Mary free

Words: 15th cent.

C. HUBERT H. PARRY
(1848–1918)